100
BASKETBALL
LEGENDS

100 Inspiring Biographies of NBA Legends and the Greatest Basketball Players of All Time

PRESENTATION

This book is part of the **WORLD STORIES ENCYCLOPEDIA series**, an important Italian-American publishing project specialized in publications for children and teenagers, and suitable for curious people of all ages.

The series includes various books with a fascinating selection of **incredible stories, facts and curiosities about society, various sports, animals, nature, science.**

All achieved with the help and advice of **industry experts** to always provide high quality information and content.

The even more attractive thing is that through these books children and teenagers will perfect their cognitive and logical skills simply by having fun.

What's more beautiful?
Happy reading and have fun friends.

The 100 Legends of BASKETBALL

1. Michael Jordan
2. LeBron James
3. Kareem Abdul-Jabbar
4. Magic Johnson
5. Larry Bird
6. Wilt Chamberlain
7. Shaquille O'Neal
8. Hakeem Olajuwon
9. Tim Duncan
10. Kobe Bryant
11. Bill Russell
12. Oscar Robertson
13. Karl Malone
14. Moses Malone
15. Dirk Nowitzki
16. Jerry West
17. Kevin Durant
18. David Robinson
19. Charles Barkley
20. Karl-Anthony Towns
21. Elgin Baylor
22. Scottie Pippen
23. George Gervin
24. Dwyane Wade

25. John Stockton
26. Kevin Garnett
27. Isiah Thomas
28. Chris Paul
29. Clyde Drexler
30. Patrick Ewing
31. Allen Iverson
32. Bob Cousy
33. Dominique Wilkins
34. James Harden
35. Paul Pierce
36. Chris Webber
37. Tracy McGrady
38. Russell Westbrook
39. Dwight Howard
40. Pau Gasol
41. Kevin McHale
42. Ray Allen
43. Reggie Miller
44. Vince Carter
45. Giannis Antetokounmpo
46. Paul George
47. Steve Nash
48. Dennis Rodman
49. Chris Bosch
50. George Mikan
51. Kawhi Leonard

52. Anthony Davis
53. Tony Parker
54. Alonzo Mourning
55. Yao Ming
56. Manu Ginobili
57. Grant Hill
58. Bernard King
59. Bob McAdoo
60. Chris Mullin
61. Dave Cowens
62. Joe Dumars
63. John Havlicek
64. Lenny Wilkens
65. Dominique Wilkins
66. Reggie Miller
67. Bob Pettit
68. Adrian Dantley
69. Allen Iverson
70. Bill Walton
71. Elton Brand
72. James Worthy
73. Clyde Drexler
74. Dennis Johnson
75. Shawn Kemp
76. Gary Payton
77. Wes Unseld
78. Hal Greer

79. Artis Gilmore
80. Ben Wallace
81. Rasheed Wallace
82. Joe Johnson
83. Amar'e Stoudemire
84. Chris Webber
85. Sidney Moncrief
86. Ralph Sampson
87. Mitch Richmond
88. Billy Cunningham
89. Bob Lanier
90. Toni Kukoc
91. Kevin Johnson
92. Derrick Rose
93. Dave Bing
94. Klay Thompson
95. Ray Allen
96. Chauncey Billups
97. Stephen Curry
98. Jason Kidd
99. Dražen Petrovic
100. Pete Maravich

Michael Jordan

Michael Jordan, born February 17, 1963, is often cited as the greatest basketball player of all time. His career was extraordinarily successful, with six NBA championships won with the Chicago Bulls and five MVP (Most Valuable Player) awards. Jordan dominated on the court and transformed basketball into a global phenomenon. His rivalry with other greats of the game took basketball to new heights of popularity in the 1980s and 1990s.

A fun fact about Jordan is his brief retirement from basketball in 1993, when he decided to play professional baseball, before returning to the NBA in 1995. Off the court, Jordan is a cultural icon with his own line of shoes and still influences the world of basketball.

LeBron James

LeBron James, born December 30, 1984, is recognized as one of the most talented and versatile players in basketball history. Entering the NBA straight out of high school, James was the first overall pick in the 2003 NBA Draft by the Cleveland Cavaliers. He won four NBA titles with three different teams, demonstrating his ability to lead and adapt to different team contexts.

In addition to his skills on the court, LeBron is known for his commitment to social work and education. He founded the "I PROMISE School" in Akron, Ohio, to help at-risk students, highlighting his commitment to underserved communities. James is also a civil rights activist and has used his platform to speak out on social justice issues.

Kareem Abdul-Jabbar

Kareem Abdul-Jabbar, born Ferdinand Lewis Alcindor Jr. on April 16, 1947, is an NBA legend with an unparalleled track record. He won six NBA titles and six regular season MVPs. His signature move, the "skyhook", was virtually impossible to stop and remains one of the most effective shots in basketball history.

Abdul-Jabbar is known not only for his performances on the field but also for his social and cultural activism. He has always had a strong commitment to civil rights and education, using his platform to promote cultural understanding and social justice. Beyond basketball, he is a prolific writer and cultural commentator, contributing literary works and articles on various social and political issues.

Magic Johnson

Earvin "Magic" Johnson Jr., born August 14, 1959, is a basketball icon known for his spectacular playing style and charismatic personality. Magic made a groundbreaking impact in the NBA, playing primarily for the Los Angeles Lakers. With his unusual height for a point guard (2,06 m), he has redefined the role, combining passing ability and game vision with physical versatility. He won five NBA championships and three MVPs.

Magic is also known for his rivalry with Larry Bird, which helped revive interest in the NBA in the 1980s. In addition to basketball, Magic is known for his entrepreneurial activity and his commitment to raising awareness of HIV after announcing his HIV status in 1991.

Larry Bird

Larry Bird, born December 7, 1956, is often remembered as one of the greatest shooters and team players in basketball history. Bird spent his entire NBA career with the Boston Celtics, leading them to three NBA championships and earning three straight MVPs. Bird was known for his incredible work ethic, shooting accuracy and game intelligence.

Bird had an unstoppable competitive spirit. During the three-point contest at the 1986 NBA All-Star Weekend, Bird walked into the locker room, looked around and simply asked, "Who goes second?", a testament to his extraordinary level of confidence. Off the field, Bird continued to influence the game as a coach and executive.

Wilt Chamberlain

Wilt Chamberlain, born August 21, 1936, and passed away October 12, 1999, was one of the most dominant and influential players in NBA history. With his imposing stature (2,16m) and athletic strength, Chamberlain set numerous records that still stand today. Including the 100 points scored in a single game in 1962.

Chamberlain was known for his colourful lifestyle and charismatic personality. He played for the Philadelphia/San Francisco Warriors, Philadelphia 76ers and Los Angeles Lakers, winning two NBA championships. Chamberlain also pioneered the use of strength and athleticism at the center position. Outside of basketball, Chamberlain was a track and field enthusiast and even participated in volleyball competitions after retiring from basketball.

Shaquille O'Neal

Shaquille O'Neal, commonly known as "Shaq", born March 6, 1972, is one of the most dominant centers the game of basketball has ever seen. His combination of size, strength and agility was unprecedented. O'Neal won four NBA titles, three of them with the Los Angeles Lakers and one with the Miami Heat. Off the court, Shaq is known for his personality, which has led to success in the worlds of entertainment and business.

One of Shaq's most memorable stories involves his partnership with Kobe Bryant on the Lakers. Despite their tensions and differences, together they formed one of the most formidable duos in NBA history. O'Neal is also known for his philanthropic work, particularly his commitment to children and education.

Hakeem Olajuwon

Hakeem Olajuwon, born January 21, 1963, in Nigeria, is universally recognized as one of the most skilled centers in the history of basketball. Known for his signature move, the "Dream Shake", Olajuwon combined excellent defence with a fluid and versatile attack. He led the Houston Rockets to two consecutive NBA championships in 1994 and 1995 and won two NBA Finals MVPs.

Interestingly, Olajuwon only started playing basketball at the age of 15, after playing football during his childhood in Nigeria, which gave him extraordinary agility and coordination for his height. After retiring, he became a respected mentor to younger players, sharing his knowledge of the game.

Tim Duncan

Tim Duncan, born April 25, 1976, in the US Virgin Islands, is often described as the "Big Fundamental" for his impeccable technical ability and efficient playing style. Duncan spent his entire 19-year career with the San Antonio Spurs, winning five NBA titles and two MVPs.

Interestingly, Duncan initially aspired of becoming an Olympic swimmer. His transition from swimming to basketball came after Hurricane Hugo destroyed his training pool in the Virgin Islands. As a player, Duncan was known for his consistency and ability to perform under pressure, becoming a model of longevity and success in the NBA.

Kobe Bryant

Kobe Bryant, born on August 23, 1978, and tragically passed away on January 26, 2020, was a Los Angeles Lakers legend and one of the most talented and respected players in basketball history. Nicknamed "Black Mamba" for his relentless mentality and work ethic, Bryant won five NBA championships and two NBA Finals MVPs during his career. He was known for his phenomenal offensive prowess and his ability to score in any situation.

Bryant grew up in Italy, where his father played basketball professionally, and developed an early love for the game. Off the court, Kobe was known for his interest in arts and culture, even winning an Oscar for his animated short film "Dear Basketball"

Bill Russell

Bill Russell, born February 12, 1934, is an iconic figure in the world of basketball, known as much for his social activism as his skills on the court. He won a record 11 NBA championships in 13 seasons with the Boston Celtics, becoming one of the greatest winners in professional sports history. His defence and rebound control were revolutionary, changing the way basketball was played.

Russell was also a pioneer in the field of civil rights, using his platform to fight against racism and promote social justice. His leadership on and off the field has been a source of inspiration for generations of athletes and activists.

Oscar Robertson

Oscar Robertson, also known as "The Big O", born November 24, 1938, is considered one of the greatest players of all time. Robertson was the first player in NBA history to average a triple-double for an entire season, a feat that defined his versatility and skill. He played for the Cincinnati Royals and Milwaukee Bucks, winning an NBA championship with the latter team.

Robertson is also known for his role in changing free agency and working conditions for NBA players, thanks to his legal battle, known as the "Robertson Case", which led to the reform of free agency and the of salaries in the league.

Karl Malone

Karl Malone, nicknamed "The Mailman", born July 24, 1963, is one of the best scorers in NBA history. He spent most of his career with the Utah Jazz, forming one of the most famous duos of all time with John Stockton. Malone won two regular season MVPs and, despite never winning an NBA championship, is recognized for his consistency and longevity.

One of Malone's defining characteristics was his exceptional physical fitness, which allowed him to maintain a high level of play well beyond the typical retirement age for most players. Malone is also known for his work ethic and dedication to constant improvement.

Moses Malone

Moses Malone, born on March 23, 1955, and passed away on September 13, 2015, was one of the greatest centers in NBA history. he was one of the first players to go directly from high school to the NBA, setting a precedent for many others. Malone won three regular season MVPs and led the Philadelphia 76ers to the 1983 NBA championship.

Malone was known for his dominance under the boards and his ability to score points, as well as his resilience and durability. He had a significant impact on how centers played, with his combination of strength and agility. Off the field, Malone was known for his humble nature and commitment to the community.

Dirk Nowitzki

Dirk Nowitzki, born June 19, 1978, in Germany, is one of the most influential European players in NBA history. With a career spanning 21 seasons, all spent with the Dallas Mavericks, Nowitzki revolutionized the power forward role with his exceptional three-point shooting and long-range ability. He won the NBA championship in 2011, earning the Finals MVP award, and received an MVP award.

A fun fact about Nowitzki concerns his path to becoming a basketball player. You started out as a tennis and handball player before dedicating yourself fully to basketball. His work ethic and dedication to continuous improvement have left an indelible mark on basketball, inspiring many European players to follow in his footsteps.

Jerry West

Jerry West, born May 28, 1938, is known as "Mr. Clutch" for his extraordinary skill at crucial moments of games. He spent his entire career with the Los Angeles Lakers, becoming one of the best guard players in NBA history. West won an NBA championship in 1972 and was a 14-time All-Star. Curiously, his silhouette has been adopted as the official logo of the NBA, making him an iconic symbol of the game.

West was also a successful executive, helping build dynasties with the Lakers and Golden State Warriors. His ability to evaluate talent and build winning teams has had a lasting impact on the league.

Kevin Durant

Kevin Durant, born September 29, 1988, is known for his incredible scoring ability and versatility. He won two NBA championships with the Golden State Warriors and two NBA Finals MVPs. Durant is unique for his combination of height, shooting ability, and agility, making him one of the hardest players to guard in the league.

Durant began his career with the Seattle SuperSonics (later Oklahoma City Thunder), where he quickly made his mark as one of the league's top scorers. He is also known for his social commitment and philanthropic activities, particularly in his hometown of Washington, DC

David Robinson

David Robinson, nicknamed "The Admiral", born August 6, 1965, is one of the greatest centers in NBA history. He spent his entire career with the San Antonio Spurs, winning two NBA championships and a regular season MVP. Robinson is known for his extraordinary defensive ability and clean play.

Before joining the NBA, Robinson served in the US Navy, which is where his nickname comes from. Off the field, he is known for his community involvement and philanthropy, particularly in education, through the founding of Carver Academy in San Antonio.

Charles Barkley

Charles Barkley, born February 20, 1963, is one of the most charismatic and polarizing players in the NBA. Despite his relatively modest height for an interior position player (6 feet 6 inches), Barkley was known for his extraordinary physical strength and rebounding ability. He won a regular season MVP in 1993 and reached the NBA Finals with the Phoenix Suns.

Barkley is as well known for his play on the field as he is for his personality off the field. he became a widely followed sports commentator, known for his straightforward opinions and sense of humour. His post-NBA career as an analyst and media personality further cemented his legacy as one of the most recognizable and influential figures in the world of basketball.

Karl-Anthony Towns

Karl-Anthony Towns, born November 15, 1995, is one of the NBA's emerging talents. Selected with the first overall pick in the 2015 NBA Draft by the Minnesota Timberwolves, Towns has quickly established himself as one of the most versatile centers in the league. he is known for his ability to score both inside and outside the box, as well as his expertise in rebounding and defensive play.

Towns made an immediate impact in the NBA, winning Rookie of the Year honours and 2016. Has setting several team records for the Timberwolves. Off the court, Towns is actively involved in philanthropic endeavours and has been outspoken on social issues, earning respect as both a player and a person.

Elgin Baylor

Elgin Baylor, born September 16, 1934, and passed away March 22, 2021, was one of the most talented and innovative players in NBA history. He spent most of his career with the Minneapolis/Los Angeles Lakers, becoming a legend for his spectacular playing style and incredible athletic abilities. Baylor was an 11-time All-Star and reached eight NBA Finals, although he never managed to win a championship.

Baylor was a pioneer in his approach to the game, with an aerial style of play that anticipated future generations of players. he was also one of the first players to speak out against racism and social injustice, using his platform to advocate for change.

Scottie Pippen

Scottie Pippen, born September 25, 1965, is widely recognized as one of the best small forward players in NBA history. He played primarily for the Chicago Bulls, forming one of basketball's most dominant duos with Michael Jordan, and helped win six NBA championships. Pippen was known for his versatility, excelling on both offense and defence.

His rise from little Central Arkansas to the NBA is a story of perseverance and dedication. Pippen stood out for his defensive prowess, winning numerous honours, and earning a spot on the NBA All-Defensive First Team for eight consecutive seasons. Since retiring, Pippen has remained an influential figure in the basketball world, both as an analyst and as an ambassador for the game.

George Gervin

George Gervin, known as "The Iceman", born April 27, 1952, was one of the best scorers in the history of the NBA and ABA. He played primarily for the San Antonio Spurs, becoming known for his smooth shot and calm under pressure, which earned him his nickname. Gervin won four NBA scoring titles and was selected to the All-Star Game 12 times.

One of his most famous moves was the "finger roll", a shooting technique near the basket that was both effective and aesthetically pleasing. Gervin was a pioneer in his fluid and flowing style of play, influencing many players who came after him.

Dwyane Wade

Dwyane Wade, born January 17, 1982, is considered one of the best guard players in NBA history. He spent the majority of his career with the Miami Heat, leading them to three NBA championships and earning Finals MVP honours in 2006. Known as "Flash" for his speed and athleticism, Wade was known for his scoring ability , create play and defend at a high level.

Wade's story is one of overcoming adversity, growing up in a tough environment in Chicago and overcoming numerous injuries throughout his career. he is also highly respected for his commitment to charity work and community support, as well as being a role model for young players.

John Stockton

John Stockton, born March 26, 1962, is considered one of the best point guards in NBA history. He spent his entire 19-year career with the Utah Jazz, setting NBA records for assists and steals that still stand today. His partnership with Karl Malone was one of the most prolific in basketball history, known for their almost telepathic pick-and-roll.

Stockton was known for his durability, game intelligence and passing accuracy. Despite his relatively modest stature and quiet appearance, he was a relentless competitor and quiet leader. Off the pitch, Stockton has always been reserved, preferring to let his performances on the parquet do the talking.

Kevin Garnett

Kevin Garnett, born May 19, 1976, is one of the most versatile interior position players in NBA history. He began his career with the Minnesota Timberwolves, becoming the first player to go directly from high school to the NBA in 20 years. Garnett was known for his defensive intensity, rebounding ability and offensive versatility.

He won an NBA championship with the Boston Celtics in 2008 and the regular season MVP award in 2004. Garnett also made a significant impact on the game with his energy and passion, becoming a role model for younger players.

Isiah Thomas

Isiah Thomas, born April 30, 1961, is remembered as one of the best point guards in NBA history. He played his entire career with the Detroit Pistons, leading them to two consecutive NBA championships in 1989 and 1990. Thomas was known for his dribbling ability, his control of the game, and his competitiveness.

Despite his modest stature, Thomas was a giant on the field, known for his resilience and fighting spirit. Off the field, Thomas has been involved in numerous business and philanthropic ventures, contributing to the community in a variety of ways.

Chris Paul

Chris Paul, born May 6, 1985, is widely considered one of the best point guards of his generation. He played for several teams in his career, including the New Orleans Hornets, Los Angeles Clippers, Houston Rockets, and Phoenix Suns. Paul is known for his excellent game control, passing, and defending ability.

Paul has made a significant impact both on and off the court, serving as president of the NBA Players Association and using his platform to advocate for social change. he is also renowned for his leadership and tactical acumen, making him one of the most respected players in the league.

Clyde Drexler

Clyde Drexler, born June 22, 1962, was one of the NBA's brightest stars in the 1980s and 90. Has spent most of his career with the Portland Trail Blazers before moving on to the Houston Rockets, where he won his only championship NBA in 1995. Nicknamed "Clyde the Glide" for his grace and athleticism, Drexler was known for his scoring prowess and defence.

Drexler was a complete player, skilled both offensively and defensively, and his elegant and effective playing style made him one of the most exciting players to watch. After retiring, he remained active in the basketball world as a coach and commentator.

Patrick Ewing

Patrick Ewing, born August 5, 1962, in Jamaica, is one of the most dominant centers in NBA history. He spent most of his career with the New York Knicks, becoming an iconic figure in New York. Ewing was known for his commanding presence under the basket, both offensively and defensively. He won Rookie of the Year in 1986 and was selected to 11 All-Star Games.

Despite never winning an NBA championship, Ewing is remembered for his leadership and impact on the court. He left an indelible mark on the league with his work ethic and dedication to the game. After retiring, Ewing became a successful coach, continuing to influence the game of basketball.

Allen Iverson

Allen Iverson, born June 7, 1975, was one of the NBA's most electrifying and polarizing players. Notoriously one of the smallest players on the court (6 feet), Iverson was known for his aggressive playing style and scoring ability. He won the regular season MVP award in 2001 and led the Philadelphia 76ers to the NBA Finals that same year.

Iverson was a major cultural figure, known as much for his impact on the court as he was for his style and personality off the court. His uncompromising approach to the game and life made him an icon for many basketball fans.

Bob Cousy

Bob Cousy, born August 9, 1928, was one of the NBA's first great point guards. He spent most of his career with the Boston Celtics, winning six NBA championships and being selected to 13 All-Star Games. Cousy was known for his excellent ball control, passing skills and game vision.

Cousy played a fundamental role in the evolution of basketball, bringing creativity and spectacularity to the point guard role. Even after retirement, he remained an influential figure in the world of basketball, contributing to the development of the game.

Dominique Wilkins

Dominique Wilkins, born January 12, 1960, is known as "The Human Highlight Film" for his spectacular dunks and athletic playing style. He spent most of his career with the Atlanta Hawks, becoming one of the best scorers in the NBA. Wilkins was selected to nine All-Star Games and won two NBA All-Star Weekend dunk contests.

Wilkins was known for his ability to score in many different ways, both with high jumps and long range shots. His athleticism and showmanship left an indelible mark on the league.

James Harden

James Harden, born August 26, 1989, is recognized as one of the best scorers and point guards of his generation. He began his NBA career with the Oklahoma City Thunder before becoming a superstar with the Houston Rockets. Harden is known for his play-creating ability, his three-point shooting and his ability to get to the line regularly.

Harden won the regular season MVP award in 2018 and led the league in points for several years. he was also a pioneer in using innovative movements and steps to create space and score, influencing the way the game is played today.

Paul Pierce

Paul Pierce, born October 13, 1977, is known as one of the clutch players in the NBA, nicknamed "The Truth". He spent most of his career with the Boston Celtics, becoming an icon of the team and leading them to the NBA championship in 2008, where he was named Finals MVP. His career was characterized by exceptional offensive play, including his ability to shoot three-pointers and in isolation situations.

Pierce is also known for his extraordinary resilience, especially after returning to the court during the 2008 NBA Finals after what appeared to be a serious injury. Off the court, Pierce became a sports commentator and continues to be an influential figure in basketball.

Chris Webber

Chris Webber, born March 1, 1973, was one of the most talented interior position players of his generation. Selected with the first overall pick in the 1993 NBA Draft, Webber had a successful career with teams such as the Golden State Warriors, Washington Bullets/Wizards, Sacramento Kings, and others. He was known for his versatility, passing ability and aerial play.

His career was marked by standout moments, including leading the Sacramento Kings to several successful playoff games. However, his career has also been accompanied by controversies, including that relating to his time at the University of Michigan as part of the famous "Fab Five". Webber is also known for his work as a basketball analyst and commentator.

Tracy McGrady

Tracy McGrady, born May 24, 1979, was one of the most talented and versatile players of his era. He played for several teams, including the Toronto Raptors, Orlando Magic, and Houston Rockets, demonstrating remarkable scoring ability and athletic versatility. McGrady was a seven-time All-Star and two-time NBA leading scorer.

His career was characterized by extraordinary performances, including some of the most memorable comebacks in NBA history. However, his individual exploits never translated into playoff success, partly due to injuries. After retiring, McGrady became a respected basketball analyst.

Russell Westbrook

Russell Westbrook, born November 12, 1988, is known for his explosive playing style and extraordinary athleticism. He began his NBA career with the Oklahoma City Thunder, where he became the second player in NBA history to average a triple-double for a full season, a feat he repeated in several subsequent seasons. Westbrook won the regular season MVP award in 2017.

In addition to his performances on the field, Westbrook is known for his unique fashion style and his commitment to philanthropy, with a focus on education and supporting children. His vibrant personality and aggressive approach to the game have left an indelible mark on the world of basketball.

Dwight Howard

Dwight Howard, born December 8, 1985, was one of the most dominant centers of his generation, particularly known for his defence and aerial play. Selected with the first overall pick in the 2004 NBA Draft by the Orlando Magic, Howard quickly earned recognition as one of the league's best defenders, winning the NBA Defensive Player of the Year three years in a row.

Howard led the Orlando Magic to the NBA Finals in 2009 and played for several other teams, including the Los Angeles Lakers, with whom he won his first NBA championship in 2020. Despite some controversies and transfers throughout his career, the Howard's impact on the court was unquestionable, especially in his ability to rebound and block opposing shots.

Pau Gasol

Pau Gasol, born July 6, 1980, in Barcelona, is one of the most influential and respected European players in the history of the NBA. Since beginning his career in 2001, Gasol has quickly made his mark as one of the most skilled and versatile centers in the league. He won the Rookie of the Year award, becoming the first non-American player to earn this recognition.

His ability to score, both with effective shots near the basket and his mid-range play, along with his excellent game vision and passing ability, made him a key player on those winning teams. In addition to his skills on the field, Gasol is known for his humanitarian and health work. He also had a huge impact on international basketball, leading the Spanish national team to numerous successes.

Kevin McHale

Kevin McHale, born December 19, 1957, ain Hibbing, Minnesota, is considered one of the best interior position players in NBA history. He spent his entire 13-year career with the Boston Celtics. McHale was selected to seven All-Star Games and won three NBA championships with the Celtics in the 1980s.

McHale was known for his exceptional defensive skills, twice winning the NBA's Best Sixth Man award. His ability to play under the basket, combined with his exceptional game intelligence and passing ability, made him a formidable opponent. Off the field, McHale continued to influence the game as a coach and executive, helping to develop new generations of players.

Ray Allen

Ray Allen, born July 20, 1975, is universally recognized as one of the best three-point shooters in NBA history. With a career spanning 18 seasons and multiple teams, including the Milwaukee Bucks, Seattle SuperSonics, Boston Celtics and Miami Heat, Allen has made a name for himself as one of the league's deadliest snipers. He set the NBA record for most three-point shots in a career.

Allen has won two NBA championships, and is most notably known for his crucial shot in Game 6 of the 2013 NBA Finals against the San Antonio Spurs, a moment that has become one of the most memorable in recent NBA history.

He has also made a significant impact off the field by engaging in philanthropic activities.

Reggie Miller

Reggie Miller, born August 24, 1965, in Riverside, California, is considered one of the greatest shooters in NBA history. He spent his entire 18-year career with the Indiana Pacers. Miller is known for his decisive shots which have earned him a reputation as one of the clutch players in basketball. Miller set numerous records, including the most playoff three-pointers made in NBA history up to that point.

Miller is also known for his intense rivalry with the New York Knicks and especially Spike Lee, which led to some of the most memorable and spectacular moments in NBA playoff history. After retiring, Miller became a successful television commentator.

Vince Carter

Vince Carter, born January 26, 1977, is celebrated as one of the most athletic and spectacular players in NBA history. His 22-season career was marked by memorable moments and breathtaking dunks, earning him the nickname "Vinsanity." Carter is known for his victory in the 2000 NBA All-Star Weekend Slam Dunk Contest, considered by many to be one of the best dunk contests of all time.

Throughout his career, Carter played for various teams, and off the court, Carter was active in various philanthropic initiatives and mentorship programs, contributing to the growth and development of basketball globally. His legacy in basketball is not just limited to his athletic abilities, but also his impact as an ambassador for the game.

Giannis Antetokounmpo

Giannis Antetokounmpo, born December 6, 1994, in Athens, Greece, has quickly become one of the most dominant and versatile players in the NBA. Known as "The Greek Freak" for his extraordinary combination of height, length, and athleticism, Antetokounmpo began his NBA career with the Milwaukee Bucks and won two consecutive regular season MVPs, as well as leading the Bucks to the NBA title in 2021 .

Antetokounmpo is known for his uncanny ability to play multiple positions, from guard to center, demonstrating prowess on both offense and defence. His personal story is equally remarkable, having grown up in poverty in Greece and fought his way to citizenship to become an international superstar.

Paul George

Paul George, born May 2, 1990, a, Palmdale, California, is a professional basketball player known for his versatility and defensive skills. He began his NBA career with the Indiana Pacers, becoming one of the best small forward players in the league.

George's career was marred by a serious leg injury in 2014, which many feared could jeopardize his basketball future. However, his incredible resilience and determination led to a remarkable recovery and return to playing at a high level. After playing for the Oklahoma City Thunder, George joined the Los Angeles Clippers, forming one of the league's strongest duos with Kawhi Leonard.

Steve Nash

Steve Nash, born February 7, 1974, in South Africa and raised in Canada, is one of the best point guards in NBA history. Throughout his career, especially with the Phoenix Suns, Nash has shown off his incredible vision of the game. He won two consecutive regular season MVPs, becoming one of the few players in NBA history to earn such recognition.

Nash revolutionized the point guard role, combining excellent ball control with a team-oriented mentality. Leadership and ability to create scoring opportunities helped define the Suns' modern run-and-gun style of play. After retiring he remained active in the basketball world as a coach and as an influential voice in promoting basketball.

Dennis Rodman

Dennis Rodman, born May 13, 1961, in Trenton, is one of the most colourful and controversial players in NBA history. Known as much for his eccentric behaviour off the court as his exceptional defensive and rebounding skills on the court, Rodman had a successful career, winning five NBA championships and earning the NBA Defensive Player of the Year award twice.

His rebounding ability, despite his relative lack of height and physical strength for an interior role player, was exceptional. Rodman is also known for his unique personality, which included colourful hair, flashy tattoos, and often unpredictable behaviour.

Chris Bosch

Chris Bosh, born March 24, 1984, in Dallas, was a key player in the NBA, known for his versatility and offensive skills. He began his career with the Toronto Raptors, where he established himself as one of the best interior position players in the league. Bosh then formed, together with LeBron James and Dwyane Wade, the famous "Big Three" of the Miami Heat, winning two NBA championships.

Bosh was known for his ability to score both near the basket and outside the basket, a rarity for a player of his height. His career was unfortunately shortened by health issues related to blood clots, which forced him to retire from professional basketball prematurely.

George Mikan

George Mikan, born on June 18, 1924, and passed away on June 1, 2005, is often considered the first great center in the history of basketball and one of the pioneers of the modern game. Playing primarily for the Minneapolis Lakers in the 1940s and 1950s, Mikan dominated the league with his height (2,06 m) and skills under the basket.

Mikan was known for his physical strength, his play under the basket and his ability to score, so much so that NBA had to change some rules to balance his dominance, such as the introduction of the three-second free throw. He also played a key role in the founding of the American Basketball Association (ABA), contributing significantly to the growth and popularity of professional basketball.

Kawhi Leonard

Kawhi Leonard, born June 29, 1991, is a professional basketball player known for his impressive defensive ability and his quiet but effective game. He began his NBA career with the San Antonio Spurs, where he won an NBA championship and Finals MVP award in 2014. Leonard was also instrumental in leading the Toronto Raptors to their first NBA title in 2019, earning the title again of Finals MVP.

His ability to play defensively, combined with his growing effectiveness on offense, has made him one of the most complete and feared players in the league. Leonard is known for his work ethic, his calm approach to the game and his ability to execute in crucial moments.

Anthony Davis

Anthony Davis, born March 11, 1993, is one of the most versatile and dominant talents in the NBA. Selected with the first overall pick in the 2012 NBA Draft by the New Orleans Hornets (now Pelicans), Davis quickly established himself as one of the best interior position players in the league. he is known for his combination of size, athletic ability, and talent on both offense and defence.

Davis won his first NBA championship with the Los Angeles Lakers in 2020, playing a crucial role alongside LeBron James. His ability to block shots, rebound and score makes him a key player on any team. Off the court, Davis is known for his community involvement and philanthropic endeavours.

Tony Parker

Tony Parker, born May 17, 1982, ain Bruges, Belgium, and raised in France, is one of the best international point guards in NBA history. He spent most of his career with the San Antonio Spurs, winning four NBA championships and earning the Finals MVP award in 2007. Parker was known for his speed, ball control, and shooting ability.

Parker played an integral role in the Spurs' dynasty of the 2000s, playing alongside Tim Duncan and Manu Gin Bili. In addition to his successes in the NBA, Parker has made a significant impact in international basketball, leading the French national team to several successes in international competitions.

Alonzo Mourning

Alonzo Mourning, born February 8, 1970, was one of the NBA's dominant centers in the 1990s and earlier 2000. Has won the NBA's Defensive Player of the Year award twice and helped lead the Miami Heat to their first NBA championship in 2006.

Mourning's career was marked by a battle with severe kidney disease, which forced him to undergo a kidney transplant in 2003. His determination and resilience in returning to professional basketball after the operation have been an inspiration to many . Off the pitch, Mourning is known for his commitment to charity work and community support.

Yao Ming

Yao Ming, born September 12, 1980, in Shanghai, China, is one of the most influential figures in international basketball. Yao made an immediate impact in the NBA with his towering stature (2,29 m) and skills around the basket. He revolutionized the center role with his combination of size, skill, and game intelligence.

Yao has become an icon in China, significantly helping to expand the NBA's popularity in the country. His career, however, was shortened by injuries, leading him to retire prematurely in 2011. Despite this, Yao's legacy in the world of basketball remains immense, not only for his performances on the court but also for his role in bridging the gap between Chinese and international basketball.

56

Manu Gin Bili

Manu Gin Bili, born July 28, 1977, in Blanca, Argentina, is one of the most decorated and beloved players in the NBA. Playing for the San Antonio Spurs throughout his NBA career, Gin Bili was instrumental to the team's success, winning four NBA championships. Known for his creative and unpredictable playing style, Gin Bili was a pioneer in bringing the art of the "Euro step" to the NBA.

His career was marked by memorable moments, including crucial shots and spectacular plays. In addition to his successes in the NBA, Gin Bili made a huge impact in international basketball, leading the Argentine national team to the gold medal at the 2004 Olympics. His retirement in 2018 has marked the end of an era for the Spurs and basketball international.

Grant Hill

Grant Hill, born October 5, 1972, in Dallas, Texas, was one of the most promising talents of his generation. Selected with the third overall pick in the 1994 NBA Draft by the Detroit Pistons, Hill made an immediate impact on the league, sharing Rookie of the Year honours with Jason Kidd. He was known for his versatility, scoring, passing, and rebounding abilities, earning comparisons to greats like Michael Jordan and LeBron James.

Hill's career was unfortunately marred by a series of serious injuries that limited his potential. However, he has shown remarkable resilience, returning to play at a high level with the Phoenix Suns and Orlando Magic. Hill is also recognized for his playing intelligence, his character, and his community commitment.

Bernard King

Bernard King, born December 4, 1956, in Brooklyn, New York, was one of the NBA's best scorers in the 1980s. King was known for his ability to score in a variety of ways, both with jump shots and aggressive drives to the basket. He had his best years with the New York Knicks, where he set numerous team records and left an indelible mark on franchise history.

King has dealt with several serious injuries throughout his career, but has managed to return to playing at a high level, demonstrating incredible determination and willpower. He is remembered as one of the most talented and resilient players of his era, and his election into the Basketball Hall of Fame in 2013 was a testament to his impact on the game.

Bob McAdoo

Bob McAdoo, born September 25, 1951, in Greensboro, North Carolina, was one of the most dominant players of the 1970s. McAdoo quickly made his mark as one of the league's best scorers. He won the regular season MVP award in 1975 and led the league in scoring for three consecutive seasons.

McAdoo was a versatile player, capable of playing both as a power forward and as a center. His ability to shoot from mid-range and his play under the basket made him a formidable opponent. He also won two NBA championships with the Los Angeles Lakers in the 1980s, adding another dimension to his already impressive career. After retiring, McAdoo continued to be involved in basketball as a coach and scout.

Chris Mullin

Chris Mullin, born July 30, 1963, in Brooklyn, New York, was one of the best shooters and team players in NBA history. Mullin became a key piece of the famed "Run TMC" Warriors alongside Tim Hardaway and Mitch Richmond. He was known for his shooting accuracy, his game intelligence, and his dedication to work ethic.

Mullin was a five-time All-Star and member of the 1992 Olympic "Dream Team," helping win the gold medal. In addition to his skills on the court, Mullin has been an example of resilience, overcoming personal issues and becoming an impact player both in the NBA and internationally. After retiring, he was active as an executive and coach, influencing the game from off the pitch.

Dave Cowens

Dave Cowens, born October 25, 1948, in Newport, Kentucky, was one of the most unique and versatile centers of his era. Playing for the Boston Celtics during the 1970s, Cowens was known for his intensity, defensive commitment, and rebounding ability. Despite his relatively modest stature for a center, his work ethic and grit made up for it, making him a key player for the Celtics.

Cowens helped the Celtics win two NBA championships and won the regular season MVP award in 1973. He was selected to seven All-Star Games and left an indelible mark on the history of the Celtics and the NBA with his style of unique play and its leadership.

Joe Dumars

Joe Dumars, born May 24, 1963, in Shreveport, Louisiana, was a key player in the legendary "Bad Boys" of the Detroit Pistons in the late 1980s. Known for his excellent defence and solid offensive play, Dumars played a crucial role in leading the Pistons to two consecutive NBA championships in 1989 and 1990. Has won the 1989 NBA Finals MVP award and was selected to six All-Stars Games.

Dumars was known for his class and sportsmanship, a rarity in a team known for its physical and aggressive play. After retiring, he had a successful career as an NBA executive, continuing to influence the game from off the court.

John Havlicek

John Havlicek, born on April 8, 1940, and passed away on April 25, 2019, was one of the most beloved and successful players in the history of the Boston Celtics. With a career that spanned 16 years, all with the Celtics, Havlicek won eight NBA championships, helping solidify the Celtics' dynasty. He was known for his inexhaustible energy, his versatility and his skill in both offense and defence.

Havlicek remained famous for his play "Havlicek steals the ball!" during the 1965 Eastern Conference Finals, one of the most iconic moments in NBA history. His energetic playing style and his ability to play multiple roles on the field have made him a key player and an example for future generations.

Lenny Wilkens

Lenny Wilkens, born October 28, 1937, in Brooklyn, is one of the greatest coaches and players in NBA history. Wilkens was an excellent point guard, known for his vision of the game and his control of the ball. He played primarily for the St. Louis Hawks and Seattle SuperSonics, earning nine All-Star Game selections, and leaving a lasting impression as one of the best point guards of his era.

Following his playing career, Wilkens had tremendous success as a coach, winning an NBA championship with the Seattle SuperSonics in 1979. He is one of the few in NBA history to have been inducted into the Hall of Fame as both a player and a coach, demonstrating his versatility and impact both on the pitch and off the bench.

Dominique Wilkins

Dominique Wilkins, born January 12, 1960, in Paris, is universally recognized as one of the most spectacular spikers in NBA history. Known as "The Human Highlight Film," Wilkins spent the majority of his career with the Atlanta Hawks. His ability to dunk with power and creativity, combined with his ability to score in a variety of ways, has made him one of the most exciting players to watch.

Wilkins was a nine-time All-Star and won two NBA All-Star Weekend dunk contests. Although he never won an NBA title, his impact on the game was profound, influencing generations of players. After retiring, Wilkins remained an influential figure in basketball, serving as a commentator and mentor.

Reggie Miller

Reggie Miller, born August 24, 1965, in Riverside, was one of the greatest shooters and clutch players in NBA history. With a career that spanned 18 years, all with the Indiana Pacers, Miller earned a reputation as a deadly shooter, especially in crucial moments of games.

Miller finished his career with the record for most three-pointers made, a record he held for many years. His shooting ability and competitive spirit made him a formidable opponent and a player loved by fans. After retiring, Miller became a sports commentator, sharing his knowledge and passion for the game.

Bob Pettit

Bob Pettit, born December 12, 1932, in Baton Rouge, Louisiana, was one of the first great interior position players in NBA history. Pettit spent his entire career with the Milwaukee/St. Louis Hawks, becoming one of the first players to dominate under the basket. he was a two-time regular season MVP and led the Hawks to their only NBA championship in 1958.

Pettit was known for his intense work ethic and his ability to score and rebound. He set numerous scoring and rebounding records throughout his career, becoming a role model for future interior position players. After retiring, Pettit was remembered as one of the great pioneers of professional basketball.

Adrian Dantley

Adrian Dantley, born February 28, 1956, in Washington DC, was one of the greatest scorers in the NBA during the late 1970s and 1980s. Dantley, known for his ability to score in multiple ways and his shooting efficiency, spent most of his career with the Utah Jazz. He won two NBA scoring titles and was selected to six All-Star Games.

His ability to earn free throws and score efficiently made him a unique and difficult player to defend. Despite his relatively modest stature for an interior role player, Dantley was a master at creating space and finishing near the basket. After retiring, Dantley remained active in the basketball world as a coach.

Allen Iverson

Allen Iverson, born June 7, 1975, in Hampton, Virginia, is considered one of the most influential and iconic players of his era. Notoriously one of the smallest players on the court, Iverson was known for his aggressive playing style, his scoring ability, and his toughness. He spent most of his career with the Philadelphia 76ers, winning the regular season MVP award in 2001 and leading the team to the NBA Finals that same year.

Iverson was a pioneer in basketball culture and style, influencing not only the game but also fashion and hip-hop music. His tenacity, competitive spirit and authenticity made him a hero to many basketball fans and a transformative figure in the NBA. Since retiring, Iverson has remained a beloved and respected figure in the basketball world.

Bill Walton

Bill Walton, born November 5, 1952, a La Mesa, is one of the most talented and influential centers of his era, despite a career marked by injuries. Walton played for the Portland Trail Blazers, San Diego/Los Angeles Clippers, and Boston Celtics, becoming known for his excellent game intelligence, passing ability and defensive dominance.

Walton won two regular-season MVPs and was part of the 1986 champion Celtics, although he was limited by injuries throughout much of his career. In addition to his performances on the field, Walton is known for his charismatic personality and social activism. After retiring, he had a successful career as a sports commentator, loved for his unique style and passion for the game.

Elton Brand

Elton Brand, born March 11, 1979, in Cortlandt Manor, has had a successful NBA career characterized by his solid presence under the basket and his ability to score and rebound. Brand shared the Rookie of the Year award and later played for the Los Angeles Clippers, where he became a star of the team.

Brand was known for his work ethic and physical play, becoming one of the most consistent interior position players of his generation. He earned two All-Star Game selections and maintained impressive scoring and rebounding averages throughout his career. After retiring, Brand entered basketball administration, serving in various management capacities.

James Worthy

James Worthy, nicknamed "Big Game James", born February 27, 1961, in Gastonia, was one of the key players for the Los Angeles Lakers during their "Showtime" era in the 1980s. Worthy quickly established himself as an impact player, known for his speed, athleticism, and scoring ability, especially in crucial moments.

Worthy won three NBA championships with the Lakers and earned the NBA Finals MVP award in 1988. His ability to perform at the highest level in the biggest games and his chemistry with Magic Johnson and Kareem Abdul-Jabbar helped cement his place as one of basketball's greats. After retiring, Worthy became a television commentator, sharing his knowledge of the game.

Clyde Drexler

Clyde Drexler, known as "Clyde the Glide", born June 22, 1962, in New Orleans, was one of the most elegant and athletic players of his generation. Drexler spent most of his career with the Portland Trail Blazers, becoming known for his spectacular dunks and transition play.

Drexler won an NBA championship with the Houston Rockets in 1995 and was selected to 10 All-Star Games. He was known for his versatility, being able to score, pass and rebound at a high level. After retiring, Drexler had a career as a coach and commentator, remaining an influential figure in the basketball world.

Dennis Johnson

Dennis Johnson, born September 18, 1954, and passed away on February 22, 2007, was a key player for the Seattle SuperSonics and Boston Celtics teams. Johnson, earning the Finals MVP award. He later played a key role in the Celtics' success in the mid-1980s, winning two NBA championships.

Johnson was known for his outstanding defence, his leadership on the field and his ability to play well in decisive moments. Considered one of the best defenders of his era, Johnson had a profound impact on the teams he played for, not only with his statistics but also with his game intelligence and presence on the field. After retiring, Johnson continued to influence the game as a coach.

Shawn Kemp

Shawn Kemp, born November 26, 1969, in Elkhart, was one of the most athletic and spectacular players in the NBA during the 1990s. Known as "The Reign Man", Kemp spent the majority of his career with the Seattle SuperSonics. He was known for his powerful dunks and physical play, quickly becoming a fan favourite.

In addition to his athletic abilities, Kemp was an effective player on both offense and defence, contributing significantly to both aspects of the game. After leaving the SuperSonics, Kemp played for several other teams, maintaining his reputation as one of the most exciting players to watch.

Gary Payton

Gary Payton, born July 23, 1968, in Oakland, California, is considered one of the best defenders in NBA history. Nicknamed "The Glove" for his ability to "stick" to opponents like a glove, Payton spent most of his career with the Seattle SuperSonics. he was a nine-time All-Star and won the NBA Defensive Player of the Year award in 1996, becoming the first point guard to do so.

Payton was known for his intensity on the field, passing ability and aggressive defensive play. He led the SuperSonics to the 1996 NBA Finals and, near the end of his career, won a championship with the Miami Heat in 2006. In addition to his performances on the court, Payton was a charismatic and influential figure in basketball.

Wes Unseld

Wes Unseld, born March 14, 1946, and passed away June 2, 2020, was one of the most influential centers of his era. Unseld was known for his physical strength, his rebounding skills, and his excellent game vision. He won regular season MVP and Rookie of the Year in 1969, becoming one of only two players in NBA history to win both awards in the same year.

Unseld led the Bullets to the 1978 NBA championship, earning Finals MVP honours. He was known for his toughness and physical play, as well as being a quiet but effective leader on the pitch. After retiring, Unseld had a successful career as a coach and manager.

Hal Greer

Hal Greer, born June 26, 1936, and passed away April 14, 2018, was a key player for the Philadelphia 76ers (formerly the Syracuse Nationals) during the 1960s and 1970s. Greer, known for his quick and accurate jump shot, was one of the best scorers of his era. he was selected to 10 consecutive All-Star Games and helped lead the 76ers to the NBA championship in 1967.

Greer finished his career with over 20,000 points scored, becoming one of the first players to reach that milestone. His consistency and shooting ability made him a formidable opponent and a player respected by his peers. After retiring, his jersey number was retired by the 76ers, a nod to his lasting impact on the team and the league.

Artis Gilmore

Artis Gilmore, born September 21, 1949, in Chipley, was one of the most dominant centers in both the ABA and NBA. Tall 2,18 m, Gilmore was known for his dominant presence under the basket, both offensively and defensively. He began his professional career in the ABA, where he won MVP and Rookie of the Year in 1972.

After the ABA-NBA merger, Gilmore played primarily for the Chicago Bulls and San Antonio Spurs, becoming a regular All-Star and one of the league's best rebounders and shot blockers. His physical strength, combined with his ability to play under the basket, made him one of the most feared centers of his time. Gilmore was inducted into the Basketball Hall of Fame, recognizing his significant impact in both the ABA and NBA.

Ben Wallace

Ben Wallace, born September 10, 1974, in White Hall, is known as one of the most dominant defenders in NBA history. Despite going undrafted, Wallace made his mark on the league, particularly during his time with the Detroit Pistons. With an unexceptional height for a center (2,06 m), he made up for it with his incredible physical strength, athleticism, and defensive tenacity.

Wallace won the NBA Defensive Player of the Year award four times and played a key role in the Pistons' NBA championship in 2004. He was known for his ability to block shots and dominate rebounds, becoming a mainstay of the Pistons' defence .

Rasheed Wallace

Rasheed Wallace, born September 17, 1974, in Philadelphia, Pennsylvania, was one of the most versatile interior position players of his generation. Blessed with excellent shooting ability, both near the basket and from distance, Wallace had a successful career, playing for teams such as the Portland Trail Blazers, Atlanta Hawks, Detroit Pistons, and Boston Celtics.

Known for his charismatic and sometimes confrontational personality, Wallace has made a significant impact both on and off the field. He won an NBA championship with the Detroit Pistons in 2004 and holds the NBA record for most technical fouls in a season. His ability to play both attack and defence has made him a key player in the teams he has been a part of.

Joe Johnson

Joe Johnson, born June 29 in 1981 in Little Rock, Arkansas, was a player known for his offensive versatility and his ability to score in a variety of situations. He had a successful career in the NBA, playing for teams such as the Boston Celtics, Phoenix Suns, Atlanta Hawks, and Brooklyn Nets. Johnson was particularly famous for his performances in the final moments of games, earning the nickname "Iso Joe" for his ability to play in isolation.

Johnson went to seven All-Star Games and had several top seasons, most notably with the Atlanta Hawks, where he was the team's leader and leading scorer. His ability to shoot and create his own shot made him one of the most difficult players of his era to mark.

83

Amar'e Stoudemire

Amar'e Stoudemire, born November 16, 1982, in Lake Wales, was one of the most athletic and dominant centers and power forwards of the early 2000s. Stoudemire quickly proved his worth, winning the Rookie of the Year award. He was known for his powerful dunks, his play above the rim, and his ability in the pick-and-roll, particularly in conjunction with Steve Nash.

Stoudemire played a central role in the Suns' "Seven Seconds or Less" offense, helping revolutionize offensive play in the NBA. He has faced several serious injuries throughout his career, but has always come back with determination and commitment.

Chris Webber

Chris Webber, born March 1, 1973, in Detroit, was one of the most talented and versatile interior position players of his generation. Selected with the first overall pick in the 1993 NBA Draft, Webber had a successful career, playing for teams such as the Golden State Warriors, Washington Bullets/Wizards, and others. He was known for his versatility, passing ability and aerial play.

Webber's career was marked by exceptional moments, but it was also accompanied by controversies, including that surrounding his time at the University of Michigan as part of the famed "Fab Five." Webber is also known for his work as a basketball analyst and commentator.

Sidney Moncrief

Sidney Moncrief, born September 21, 1957, in Little Rock, Arkansas, was one of the NBA's toughest and most complete defenders in the 1980s. Playing primarily for the Milwaukee Bucks, Moncrief was known for his intense work ethic and prowess on defence, which earned him two consecutive NBA Defensive Player of the Year awards. In addition to his defensive skills, he was also a reliable scorer and leader on the court.

Moncrief helped lead the Bucks to several playoff appearances. His ability to contribute both offensively and defensively has made him one of the most respected and feared players in the league. After retiring, Moncrief remained active in the basketball world as a coach and mentor.

Ralph Sampson

Ralph Sampson, born July 7, 1960, in Harrisonburg, was one of the most promising and physically gifted centers when he entered the NBA. Tall 2,24 m, Sampson made an immediate impact on the league, winning Rookie of the Year and being selected to four consecutive All-Star Games. Playing for the Houston Rockets, he formed one of the most fearsome center duos with Hakeem Olajuwon, known as the "Twin Towers".

Sampson's career was marred by injuries that limited his potential. Despite this, in his healthy moments, he has demonstrated a rare combination of height, skill and versatility, significantly influencing the game as one of the first agile and multi-functional "bigs".

Mitch Richmond

Mitch Richmond, born June 30, 1965, in Fort Lauderdale, was one of the best scorers in the NBA during the 1990s. Known as "The Rock," he spent most of his career with the Sacramento Kings and Golden State Warriors, becoming known for his reliable shooting and physical strength. He was selected to six All-Star Games and won the 1996 Olympic gold medal.

Richmond has maintained a high scoring average throughout his career, proving to be one of the best offensive players. Despite playing for teams that rarely reached the playoffs, his individual skill and contributions to the game were widely recognized, culminating in his induction into the Basketball Hall of Fame.

Billy Cunningham

Billy Cunningham, born June 3, 1943, in Brooklyn, New York, was a key player for the Philadelphia 76ers in the 1960s and 1970s. Nicknamed "The Kangaroo Kid" for his incredible athleticism and leaping abilities, Cunningham was a dominant force at both small forward and power forward. He helped lead the 76ers to the NBA championship in 1967 and was selected to four All-Star Games.

Following his playing career, Cunningham had tremendous success as coach of the 76ers, winning another NBA championship in 1983. His passion for the game and his understanding of team dynamics made him a respected and influential coach, contributing to shape the future of basketball.

Bob Lanier

Bob Lanier, born September 10, 1948, in Buffalo, New York, was one of the NBA's most dominant centers in the 1970s and 1980s. Lanier was known for his ability to score, rebound and play defence. Despite playing most of his career on teams that didn't have much success in the playoffs, his individual performance was outstanding.

Lanier was selected to eight All-Star Games and maintained impressive scoring and rebounding averages throughout his career. He was known for his strength under the basket and his skill with footwork, making him one of the most feared centers of his era. Since retiring, Lanier has been active in promoting basketball and supporting various humanitarian causes.

Toni Kukoc

Toni Kukoc, born September 18, 1968, in Split, Croatia, was one of the first European players to make a significant impact in the NBA. Before joining the Chicago Bulls, Kukoc had already achieved impressive international fame, winning numerous titles and accolades in Europe. With the Bulls, he became a key part of three consecutive NBA champion teams from 1996 to 1998, known for his versatility, excellent shooting, and passing ability.

Kukoc was an interior role player unique in his ability to handle the ball, create plays and shoot three-pointers. His presence helped change the way European players were viewed in the NBA, proving that they could play a crucial role on winning teams.

Kevin Johnson

Kevin Johnson, born March 4, 1966, in Sacramento, California, was one of the best point guards in the NBA in the late 1980s and 1990s. After starting his career with the Cleveland Cavaliers, Johnson found success with the Phoenix Suns, where he spent most of his career. He was known for his dribbling ability, his speed, and his ability to score and create opportunities for teammates.

Johnson was a three-time All-Star and played a key role in leading the Suns to several playoff appearances, including the 1993 NBA Finals against the Chicago Bulls. In addition to basketball, Johnson has had a significant career in public service, serving as mayor of Sacramento.

Derrick Rose

Derrick Rose, born October 4, 1988, in Chicago, has had one of the most dynamic and tumultuous careers in the modern NBA. Rose quickly demonstrated his talent, winning the Rookie of the Year award. In 2011, he became the youngest player in NBA history to win the regular season MVP award, at age 22.

Rose was known for his incredible athleticism, speed and scoring ability. However, his career was marred by a series of serious knee injuries that limited his potential and altered the trajectory of his career. Despite these obstacles, Rose demonstrated resilience and determination, continuing to play at a high level for several teams in his later career.

Dave Bing

Dave Bing, born November 24, 1943, in Washington DC, was one of the best guard players of his generation. Selected by the Detroit Pistons in the 1966 NBA Draft, Bing became known for his scoring ability and playmaking. He was a seven-time All-Star and won the NBA's leading scorer title in 1968.

Bing was known for his leadership on the field and his commitment off the field. After his NBA career, he found success in the business world and served as mayor of Detroit, demonstrating the same dedication and leadership skills he had shown as a player.

Klay Thompson

Klay Thompson, born February 8, 1990, in Los Angeles, is one of the most accurate and lethal shooters in NBA history. Playing for the Golden State Warriors, Thompson, along with Stephen Curry, formed "The Splash Brothers", one of the most feared shooting duos in the league. He is known for his ability to score many points in short periods, setting records for most points in a quarter and most 3-pointers in a game.

Thompson played a crucial role in the Warriors' NBA championship victories, proving to be one of the team's best offensive and defensive players. His three-point shooting ability and defence have changed the way the game is played in the NBA.

Ray Allen

Ray Allen, born July 20, 1975, in Castle Air Force Base, California, is one of the best shooters in NBA history. Allen is known for his impeccable shooting technique and his ability to score from any position on the floor. He spent his career playing for several teams, including the Milwaukee Bucks, Seattle SuperSonics, Boston Celtics, and Miami Heat.

Allen was selected to ten All-Star Games and won two NBA titles, one with the Boston Celtics in 2008 and another with the Miami Heat in 2013. He is famous for his game-winning shot in Game 6 of the 2013 NBA Finals, which he helped the Miami Heat force a Game 7 and win the title. His three-point shooting ability and cool mentality in pressure situations make him a basketball legend.

Chauncey Billups

Chauncey Billups, born September 25, 1976, in Denver, Colorado, was one of the best point guards and leaders in the NBA during his career. Known as "Mr. Big Shot" for his decisive plays at crucial moments in games, Billups played for several teams, including the Detroit Pistons, Denver Nuggets and Boston Celtics.

Billups won the NBA Finals MVP award in 2004, when he led the Pistons to the NBA championship. He was known for his ability to manage the game, his three-point shooting and his leadership on the court. He participated in five All-Star Games and was a role model of leadership for his teammates.

Stephen Curry

Stephen Curry, born March 14, 1988, in Akron, Ohio, is one of the most revolutionary players in NBA history. he is known for being one of the best shooters of all time and changed the way basketball is played with his three-point shot. Curry spent his entire career with the Golden State Warriors and was a crucial part of their NBA championship wins.

Curry has won the NBA MVP award twice and has been selected to numerous All-Star Games. His ability to shoot three-pointers from incredible distances has made the Warriors one of the most dominant teams in recent years. His influence on the game is evident as many teams now try to emulate his playing style.

Jason Kidd

Jason Kidd, born March 23, 1973, in San Francisco, California, was one of the best point guards and defenders of his generation. Kidd was known for his extraordinary vision of the game, his passing ability, and his ability to read the game. He played for teams like the Phoenix Suns, New Jersey Nets and Dallas Mavericks.

Kidd was selected to twelve All-Star Games and helped the Dallas Mavericks win the NBA championship in 2011. He was also an exceptional defender, known for his steals and his ability to stop opponents. His successful career and influence in the game have made him a respected figure in the NBA.

Drazen Petrovic

Drazen Petrovic, born on October 22nd, 1964, in Ibenik, Croatia, was one of the best European basketball players of all time. He began his professional career in Europe before joining the NBA, where he played for the Portland Trail Blazers and New Jersey Nets. Petrovic was known for his incredible shooting ability and his ability to score with ease.

Unfortunately, his career was tragically cut short by a car accident in 1993, when he was only 28 years old. Petrovic had proven his talent in the NBA and had a promising future ahead of him. His untimely death was a loss to the basketball world, but his contributions to the game were commemorated with induction into the Basketball Hall of Fame and recognition as one of Europe's great basketball talents.

Pete Maravich

Pete Maravich, born June 22, 1947, in Aliquippa, Pennsylvania, was one of the most spectacular and prolific players in basketball history. He played primarily as a guard and had an outstanding college career with the LSU Tigers. Maravich has become known for his incredible dribbling skills, his sense of stage and his ability to score from any position.

In his professional career, Maravich played for the Atlanta Hawks, New Orleans Jazz, and Boston Celtics. He was selected to five All-Star Games and was the NBA's leading scorer in 1977. He is known for scoring 68 points in a single game, a record that stood for many years.

Unfortunately, Maravich's career was marred by injuries and he suffered a tragic, untimely death at just 40 years old.

Made in the USA
Columbia, SC
22 March 2025